Erasure Marks

Erasure Marks

Poems by

Mary Fox

© 2026 Mary Fox. All rights reserved.
This material may not be reproduced in any form, published,
reprinted, recorded, performed, broadcast,
rewritten or redistributed without
the explicit permission of Mary Fox.
All such actions are strictly prohibited by law.

Cover design by Shay Culligan
Cover image by Daniel Jensen on Unsplash
Author photo by Stephen Pipis of the 517 Poetry Room, 2025.

ISBN: 979-8-90146-804-3
Library of Congress Control Number: 2026931906

Kelsay Books
502 South 1040 East, A-119
American Fork, Utah 84003
Kelsaybooks.com

*This is dedicated to the memory of those I loved and lost,
and all I gained in knowing them.*

Acknowledgments

No book is ever put together without help. My help came from several sources—from Writing at the Ledges and Grand Ledge Writers, who provided feedback and suggestions; from my fellow poets Mary Anna Kruch, Margaret Krusinga, and Dennis Hinrichsen, who offered ideas to strengthen the content in meaningful ways and proffered title suggestions; from my performance friends, Masaki Takahashi and Stephen Pipis, who provided me with a photo I love and encouraged me to develop an ear for oral poetry.

Knowing how others listen and read has made me mindful of audience. And then there are my personal friends and family, who have supported me in my quest to put my life and insights fearlessly to poem. I am very grateful for them all.

Finally, thank you to the following publications, in which versions of these poems previously appeared:

East Lansing Library Poetry Contest Booklet, 2019: "Girls Athletic Association: Trip to Estes Park"
East Lansing Library Poetry Contest Booklet, 2025: "Before I Met My Tears"
Promptly Speaking, A Writing at the Ledges Anthology (Dragonfly Press, 2018): "Empty Air"
Reading Lessons (Finishing Line Press, Georgetown KY, 2019): "Dispensation," "Divorce Decree," "First Read," "In Memoriam: Christmas Greetings," "Not Unread," "Unfinished Story"
Waiting for Rain (Finishing Line Press. Georgetown, KY, 2016): "Blue-Black Chair," "Breakfast," "Grandma's Icebox," "Graveyard Melodies," Living in Limbo," "Summer's Eve, Waiting for Rain," "River Ride"

Contents

Part I: Neck deep and still want perfect

Silence	15
My Father Waits	16
My Mother Names Me	18
First Read	20
Blue-Black Chair	22
A House Divided	24
Things We Do for Love	26
Things We Cannot Hear	28
Beyond Tears	30
Graveyard Melodies	32

Part II: This moment when we breathed

River Ride	37
April Fools' Day: Annie's Birthday	39
Grandma's Icebox	41
Climbing	43
Not Unread: To Uncle Garland Who Died Young	45
This Is the Story	46
The Weight of Your Light: *In Memoriam,* Native Child	48
The Last Sunsets of Rosalie Petrouske	50
Girls Athletic Association: Trip to Estes Park, Colorado	52
Before I Met My Tears	54
Rootless	55
The Rain Within	57

Part III: Arching skyward, breathing free—untethered

Break-fast	61
All That Remains	62
Divorce Decree: Untethered	63
Closing the Door	64
Let Them Go	66
Unfinished Story	68

Part IV: Where the Twist Begins

Summer's Eve, Waiting for Rain	71
Living in Limbo	72
The Last Time We Made Love	74
Mourning in Michigan	75
Dispensation	77
In the Memory of Skin	78
Empty Air: Epitaph	80
July 4, 2020	81
In Memoriam: Christmas Greetings	82
On Layers of Grief	83
What Lingers	84
On Growing Older	85
Slow Waking	86
Erasure Marks	88
Alien Nation	90

Part I:
Neck deep and still want perfect

Silence

Frazzled memory captures
a song I could not sing
holds it in my throat
as fragile as a breath
as lonely as a lover
longed for but never met.

Sometimes a heart mourns
songs it never sang
lives never offered
but sometimes even
knowing such exists
is enough to strike a chord.

My Father Waits

Sometimes, he sat at a bar
to stare at its mirrored wall
reflecting the amber, yellows, and reds
of bottles lined against it.
There he sipped his after-work beer
and wondered: *Would she awaken?*
Still, he went each day to the auto plant
where he spray-painted cars
rolling down the line
from 2:30 to 11:00 P.M.
After, he caught the last bus home.
Bills had to be paid, though he sometimes
wished he could linger at the neighborhood bar
and drink himself numb.
In the morning, he woke early,
showered, then caught a bus to stop
at the hospital nursery to gaze through glass
at the squalling infant that was his own.
Once, he had asked to hold her,
and cradled in his arms, she stopped crying
and stared back with the bluest eyes—
like that of all infants, he was told.
Still, he recognized that wrinkle
in her forehead as his
and knew she would have eyes
of his own peculiar blue.

He had considered how she would thrive,
if her mother didn't,
then dismissed the possibility
and headed to his wife's hospital ward bed,
where she lay unconscious
and quietly hummed "Linda" to her
and whispered a reminder
that they still had music to dance to
and a new baby girl to dance with them.
He told her he loved her,
before he walked away once more
to the nursery to tell BABY SCULLY "goodnight."
Then he caught the next bus to work.

My Mother Names Me

I'd like to believe
when at my birth, my mother went
into a pre-eclampsia coma, she landed
in some limbo-heaven with her own mother,
and wearied from labor, rested
cradled in Grandma Eva's loving arms.

And I'd like to think that when my mother
considered leaving me permanently,
Grandma whispered in her ears:
"She'll be worth the trouble."
Then sometime during that week,
as she lingered, my mother shook off her longing
for her own mother and folded it small enough
and narrow enough to hold in one frayed postcard,
my grandfather had sent Grandma Eva
from some now defunct Louisiana town,
and one fading two-by-three tintype-ish photo
of Grandma Eva's face—
a near mirror-image of her own.
And she thought if those two lonely belongings
could house all her yearning for her own mother,
what kind of hunger would my rounded pink cheeks
and yellow-white hair hold for her?

Then she pulled loose from Grandma Eva's arms
and woke to name me "Mary Linda"
for a moment so bitter and beautiful.

First Read

She pools beyond my newborn eyes—
an uncertain swimmer treading water
in the churning waves before me.
We've just met, toed the water and stepped in—
just felt the sharpness of the rocky bottom,
just felt the pull of its current.
We haven't found our footing,
and neither of us wants to drown,
so we float at the mercy of the tide.

Still, I want to trust her
and the strength of her tread—
I want to lean into her cradled arms—
but I've read the quiver in her tongue
and the brine of her eyes,
and I know she is just as scared as I am.
Wearied, she wants me to just stop crying
and vomiting and fall asleep—
because she is tired and overwhelmed.
We both long to fall back
into some safe cave of slumber
where hopes become dreams
and dreams become true.

But then, I'm no baby doll,
and she's on her own
and nobody is here
to help her pretend,
and when we awaken again,
we'll be neck deep
and still want perfect.

Blue-Black Chair

From my mother's room,
I will save her bruised chair
where today she sits pulling pale stockings
over vein-stained legs.
Those legs carry her, leaning on a walker,
to her last days.

She moves more briskly than most anticipate,
so I tease her that she is training for races
we'll hold on her hundredth birthday.
Truly, I want her to slow down
and not speed too quickly to her end.

Still, I know when she dies,
I will take that bruised chair home with me,
and its old black-and-blue print will clash
with the turquoise tranquility of my home.
Yet I will find a place for it.

Later, when I miss her voice,
I will cloak myself in her chair,
conjuring her voice in reveries
and closing my eyes,
I will find her world imprinted
in its swirling pattern.

My mother would be surprised
I will take so much of her with me.
From the start, we pulled and pummeled each other.
My mother's daughter, more than my father's child,

I bear the curse of her intelligence,
will, and a too-giving heart
that carried all the worry of awareness—
its history fraught with poverty and death.
Once, I toddled across an unpaved street
to gather dandelions
growing yellow in empty-lot splendor.
Clutching their green-stemmed ooze,
I offered buttery tops to my mother.
She gathered my hands gently in hers
and conflicted, swatted my bottom
because I ventured a road
heedless of potential dangers.
I felt the sting of rejection,
and we both wept.

My mother's life bloomed
in hillsides of disease, despair, and death—
mine in the hot house of her love.
No, I will not weep for my mother.
I will know her.
A Persephone emerging from grief,
I will not spiral in sadness,
uncomforted in a world
devoid of Mother.
Cocooned in the shelter of her blue-black chair,
I will read the triumph of her life
and from the wisdom of her tales blossom—
enthroned.

A House Divided

I miss the boy you were:
   soft enough to shed a tear,
   kind enough to sell candy to help your sis,
   brave enough to fight for friends.
I'm still saddened at the way parents divided us:
   you were star and savior;
   I did the dirty work—
   cleaned up flooded basements and managed anger.
You were "toughened" up; I was boxed out—
   no room in life for a too-smart daughter wanting to star,
   no vision for that bookworm-thinker in a man's world,
   no time except for favored son, family hero.
Rootless and untethered I moved away:
   you stayed where your ties were tended—
   I planted myself and found a spot of sun and shade
   watered myself with my tears then tested other waters.
Some of us learn to raise ourselves; others have shepherds.
   I think I found the better bargain.
   I think you withered on that over-nurtured vine,
   too well trimmed and too rootbound to grow.

And here we are: fully matured yet so far apart—
  no shared ties but still standing in our truths—
  truly disconnected in time and space
  and heart.

Things We Do for Love

Friday, I take two-hour drive on
congested highways,
where cars play bump 'em
and dodge 'em in weaves I never figure out,
to take Mother to HER hairdresser
who charges less and doesn't do *that*
"weird thing" she hates with her hair
she un-greys to bright white brilliance
so that her scalp gleams pinkly through curls
and she will be 93-year-old perfect
at my brother's third wedding reception
located in a hotel near a casino,
to which he and Bride 3
have sent out invitations with rolling dice—
because it is a gamble—
to celebrate his marriage to a woman
who buys handguns and owns a carry license,
and who will probably kill him
in an accidental drunken shoot-out
some evening when he rises too often to urinate,
so while I will gleam with good wishes
and champagne-toast their future,
reassuring my just-want-everyone-happy mother,
I will take quiet sips of anxiety
and swallow my panic's insights
in silent red-wine swigs.

Later, in the smooth purple twilight,
I unbraid the way home,
recall glimpses of my brother's smile
and how they gazed into each other's eyes
and remember how he tries to please,
and as I taste a few swallows of hope,
I follow the streaked sunset
till the road turns true North
where I finally breathe.

Things We Cannot Hear

My niece hears something.
"What is that?" she asks.
I shake my head "no."
I hear nothing.
"Don't you hear that?"
I smile. I know I am fading.
Each year I give something up—
another gift I cannot retrieve:
    a walk without pain
    a book without glasses
    an evening snack without indigestion.

She stands and looks out the slider,
then suddenly opens it and runs.
I trail behind
and look down off the deck.
She snatches something from the cats
lying intent, watching her,
from the warmth of summer cement.

When I join her,
she holds a bundle of fluff,
a baby rabbit caught
by my miniature lion and panther,
who, in the sun, now stretch indifferently,
willing to give up their prize.
(They are well fed.)

"I'll take it back with me,"
she reassures me.

"It will be okay.
I'll release it in the woods."
My niece, naiad of the forest,
retrieves a box from the garage
sets the injured animal inside
and then closes the top
to its casket.
Still, I do not tell her
it is too late.
Or that cats, though quicker,
are as efficient as time.

She drives away soon after
loaded with things I've given her:
   a weekend job babysitting the cats who adore her,
   a photo of her now-dead father and his sister as toddlers
   an angel for her garden to watch over her—
   items and purrs to ground her in loving memories—
   and a bundle of fluff she will release to die
   in the woods behind her house.

Perhaps she will not notice
the burden in kindness.

Beyond Tears

My daughter weeps without tears.
Between packing sandwiches
and baking cinnamon rolls
her eyes deaden—
blind in the moment,
she mourns.

Still, she tends the summer lunch truck—
smiles and tries to lighten
summer poverty with kindness—
and a sandwich with dessert.
Yet that unfamiliar heaviness
clamps her breath—
leadens her heart.
In the day's pauses, when no eyes follow her,
she sobs silently and dryly.

At home as she tends to other lives:
her now-grown children's bewilderment,
her young grandchildren's questions,
her own grieving spouse,
but her heart demands some answer—
to why her middle son is gone at twenty-seven,
while her life plods on helpless
to reverse the days.
Tears might not continually streak her face
or dampen her pillow
but love's price floods her heart—
leaks from its beat—
in gasps—

memory surges
of what was, but is not—
and she tries not to tangle in *why*—
why she is still *here* and he is not.
She balls her hands
but still, they grasp for meaning:
  Didn't she raise her son to be
  a man of honor? A blessing for life?
  And hadn't he pursued his happiness
  found both love and purpose?
  Hadn't she celebrated his growth—
  not just in inches marked on a door frame
  but in the depth of his understanding?

Who should account for this despair—
no drunk driver, no criminal with a gun,
no bloody malfunctioning machine?
And she doesn't know why—
or truly care.
And she doesn't have it in her heart
to hate beyond reason.
  (And she just wants him back.
  She just wants him back.
  She just wants him back—
  to swipe the cowlick from his forehead
  cup his little boy face again,
  and have him in her arms
  once more.)

Graveyard Melodies

In the early chill of August dusk,
I stroll the local cemetery path
reading headstones—
summaries of lives I never knew.
With somber voices, those graveyard stones
trill wayward hymns of memory.
Off-key, discordant,
in the thick-winged flutter of moths
hovering in faint light of faded dresses
and faltering shadows,
their cacophony tangles into symphony,
a recital of wraiths in an unfamiliar church yard.

Their serenade dredges up my dead,
resurrects them in their own sad songs.
I shroud them gently with simple melodies.
I tuck in ragged edges behind the sharps and pat them
rhythmically into soothing remembrance
small enough for a headstone—
a false lullaby humming
the way things never were.
In lilting carols, frayed history repairs.

Yet even as I do, my heart rebels,
and like some wild forest bird, startles,
slips the chords, unravels its threads
and takes flight,
keening.

Part II:
This moment when we breathed

River Ride

A river is not water
but rock and reed and branch
and turn and bend, flowing,
gushing, spitting,
splashing clear,
tumbling in cloudy inches,
falling and rising
against landscape.
Moment glides to moment,
as we slide our silver paddles
to crease a wave, widen the arc,
turning—twisting in the water's flow.
We move in tandem
orchestrating our ride.
In silent conversations,
we grasp
at battered stones
or grind over gritty shallows.
Too casually, with a nod, a shrug
we chance an offshoot,
yearning for deep-water
and channeled currents
to cradle us.
Yet, with every rotation of wrist,
with each leaning of weight,
weariness overwhelms me, winds me,
chilling me in blankness—
unhinging me from the flow—

till I fear losing memory
of our ride,
this moment
where we breathed
and rocked against boulders,
trembling in our tinny haven,
knowing we were not river;
we were not fin or shell,
but other flesh and bone
rolling on our waves.

April Fools' Day: Annie's Birthday

In Sherry's dining room, we gather.
six long-time friends at Annie's birthday lunch.
I slide into the last open chair
as Annie, our birthday "girl" opens cards,
delights in reading them and accepts our small gifts.
She jokes about retail therapy as we smile and laugh.
But this day is different from other birthday gatherings.

She stares at my face. "I know you," she says,
as I hand her my card, and I try to believe her.
Today she is 74, but her mind
sifts out days and untethers time,
and sometimes loses our features.
Dementia spins like a spider,
sets traps, stems emotions,
scrambles events in its webs.
It encases our memories—
the days we wove—beyond reach
in tight untouchable cocoons of silk.

But even these threads unravel, disintegrate, dissolve
and more frequently we need each other
to patch in names or places or times.
We hold onto our flip-phone recollections
of days already lived, cling to past narratives,
our meaning, our place in time,
our mutual recollection.

Each one of us is grateful
for those fragments of memory shared by friends—

those patches that fill in what we can't recall.
So on Annie's birthday we sit with our friend
on her road to full-blown dementia
and fill in the blanks of her life and our own.

Grandma's Icebox

One Sunday, we rode the bus to visit Grandma.
My father, stoic, sat buried in a *Free Press* crossword,
inking words effortlessly as the bus staggered forward.
In her aisle seat, across from Dad, Mama gazed out the windshield,
restless in church clothes that never quite covered
her Southern drawl or Baptist roots
my Irish-Catholic grandmother despised.
My four-year-old self, warmed through my woolen coat
by my mother's soft side, pressed against the November window
breathing clouds and drawing pictures.

Factories and gritty streets chugged by.
At Kerchaval, we exited the bus then
picked our way over broken sidewalks,
past the worn brownstone facades,
careful of our step on the slippery, half-thawed patches,
until Grandma's house appeared, a chipped, bleak edifice.

Grandpa greeted us gruffly, his booming voice
so different from his taciturn son's.
In a spare bedroom, Mama laid our coats in a neat pile
while Grandpa backed into his overstuffed chair
pinned with stiff doilies, protection from the pomade
polishing his shiny black hair
We lined the couch, perched in a pinched row, waiting.
Soon, Grandpa dug into his pockets
for the silver dollars he used to fish for me,
though he lured me more with smiles and open hands.

Grandma lingered in the kitchen chipping slivers
from a block of ice for the cool, dark drinks
she then offered us in fussy, etched glasses.
We sipped them, tongues numbing,
under her chilly gaze in her wintry house,
where we shivered, even sweatered
in our heaviest clothes.

After, I carried my glass into the kitchen
where I could gaze on Grandma's icebox.
Like Grandma, her icebox was a short, wooden square,
with two compartments at heart:
In one was that block of ice,
hard and cool-blue clear as her Irish eyes.
The other never opened for me.

The bus ride home is endless—even today, I ride.
Just a glance in a mirror enfolds me in its sway—
I see my mother's smile and loose blonde waves,
my father's ink-smeared fingers,
and my grandfather's awkward, friendly reach.
Then Grandma's cool blue eyes pool back at me,
unthawed by time or place, undiminished cubes of ice
where her memory should be.

Climbing

Mama liked to sleep in, so when I entered school,
she chose to send me to afternoon kindergarten.
That was why on a cloudy, windy October morn,
I was alone when I mastered the fuel oil tank.
It sat behind Alice's house
where it stored oil for winter heat
and offered the neighborhood crew a challenge
to scale its slippery sides.
I was five years old and wrapped
in my brown corduroys and a blue fall jacket
when I stood puzzling how I'd make it to its top.
I glanced at the place where I'd seen older kids
grab battered apple crates to use for leverage.
I yanked one from a pile stacked near the garage,
turned it sideways and propped it
against the silvered legs of the tank,
then grasped the ridges of welding
rimming seams in thick layers to pull up
till I could steady my sturdy legs
against the house's gritty, gray faux-brick siding.
I pushed until my bent knees straighten,
and slid topside on my belly where I rose,
arms tugging me to the top ridge
where I could throw one leg over it
to ride its rounded body like a pony.
Later, when I caught my breath
and quieted my hammering heart,
I threw both legs forward and leaned back,
and braced against the house,
I sat as if in a Lazyboy, relaxed but proud.

A month later, in November when Uncle Garland died,
I sat there for hours ashen-faced
and wept in a winter winds' desolate chill.

Not Unread: To Uncle Garland Who Died Young

Do not think because your life was short
you were unread. My child's eyes read
you on a summer's day
when you stood me on your new red Olds.
Mother admonished you to "get me off "
before I "scratched the paint."
You laughed
then balanced two-year-old legs
on a fender slick with wax.

I was only five that day you died.
I remember the sprint
and the cold scramble
up a neighbor's heating oil tank
waiting for another kind of winter.
Only Mother could coax me down.

I am old now, much older than you.
Still, I read your letters from France and Germany.
A gunner and a sometimes cook—
I remember my mother used your recipes
and taught me your wisdom of salt.
Every day I see you with Mother,
your wife, and Grandfather
standing in pictures I hang in my hall—
You were someone I needed to know,
if only briefly—
reassurance even then
someone loved me as I was: imperfect,
off-balance and not quite formed.

This Is the Story

This is the story I've wanted to tell:
   The back of his hand brushing against my bud of a breast
   leaving me thirteen-year-old wordless
   as I stood shaken in that red-bricked classroom chill,
   confused.
   Some lost-child spirit sent an icy warning,
   shivered me in her ghostly whispers.
   Yet still, I stood possessed—
   shocked by some primal urge that surged
   trilling a flame of desire through me—
   thrumming an unfamiliar pulse of pleasure
   between my legs. It lit something threatening
   yet curious, unfamiliar but pleasurable
   that bewildered me.

The bell rang.
   He stepped back, dropped his hand
   glanced at the oaken classroom door,
   listened to the shuffling students trek
   toward their after-lunch class.
   Then anticipating some unwanted interruption,
   he shuffled quietly to flick off the classroom light
   and twist the classroom lock.
   The door's high window sent the halls lights
   through to the floor in a defined square
   as footsteps and shouting voices diminished.

Imprisoned in the shadows, I sat bewildered, placing
 a desk between me and that caressing hand
 casting its spell—
 a barrier that would not hold—
 waiting . . .

The Weight of Your Light:
In Memoriam, Native Child

I struggle to lift the weight of your absence.
How do I carry the chill of your death?
It hovers ghostly, a shivered remembrance—
a revulsion of that icy hand slicing you from our lives.
(What demon enters a man
to prompt murder of what he claims to love?
As he stabbed you, did he think:
your leaking blood would embrace him
or your cold dead body thaw his hardened heart?
As he lifted that knife 17 times
to hack away his hurt,
did that carnage comfort him?)

I struggle to carry the weight of your light.
What you taught lies in the cinders of your death
when its words should blaze a path to hope and solace.
How do I ignite messages ashen with your demise?
What words could strike their flints,
or snatch the fire back from selfish brutality?

God, help me! I struggle
to salvage that promise
from sorrow and despair.

But God help me
I cannot have your fire snuffed
when you should have lit the way.

The Last Sunsets of Rosalie Petrouske

I saw ridges of your bravery
backboned behind the unanswerable.
Your futile complaints had no happy answers.
So even though your whole life,
all you wanted was a soft place to land,
you landed in that thorny bed of cancer,
fighting for life, but still looking
for those Hallmark rose petals.

Inside, the fractures of youth—
death, poverty, prejudice,
abandonment, abuse, grief—
scarred your faith and fueled fear.
Every "what if?" repelled
the peace that you wanted.
Somehow, your desires never grasped reality.
But then, dreams hold no parameters
while reality fits in the spaces that exist.

Still, I hope those last sunsets found
something golden and warm in their shine,
that they uncovered those facets of crystal delight
and pleasures of pillow-soft comfort
in the river's flow as you walked
its familiar path bidding goodbye
to the foliage and fauna that lit your camera;

in your friends' voices as they comforted you
with shared memories of journeys,
laughter, and unexpected kindnesses;
in the bowls of potato soup they brought;
in their patience as they let you phone in
your rage at the unfairness of it all—
in that real space where they offered
the love they had because you mattered.

Girls Athletic Association:
Trip to Estes Park, Colorado

Somewhere, on our way to Estes,
we stopped our parade of cars
by a lumber company closed for the weekend.
Its emptiness called us to explore.
After the long, second-day ride from Michigan,
Bobby Jo and I freed our young limbs
and sprinted toward a pile of raw logs,
scattered like unsorted pick-up sticks
Laughing, we climbed its tumbled layers.

As the June heat warmed us,
logs swayed beneath our feet,
as if a breeze had caught them in some current.
Still Bobby Jo, more sure-footed than I, tested each step
then routed our orbit skyward in a long arch
till we reached the top-most log.
From a distance, I heard the whispers of the woods,
pure, steady, unmuddled
by the grind of machinery or the lisp of saws—
just a faint hush of air through Colorado trees.
At the top, we paused to breathe in this landscape
and its unfamiliar lightness.

On that crooked hill of scrambled trunks,
we stood in its strangeness—
unnaturally stilled by the emptiness
pocked with tree stumps
and by the flap of brush muttering
its sorrow.

Before I Met My Tears

Before I met my tears, I knew how to grieve:
    Next door, Old Bill Patterson died, so I slipped
    into his garden each morning and stole
    a strawberry, red and ripe, and biting
    through its sun-warmed seeds
    into the sweet juice of memory, I found
    him and brought back his crackly grandpa
    voice: "Now just eat one or two or
    there will be none for shortcake." Then I sat
    cross-legged on the backdoor steps, savored
    my longing for him, my honey-tart
    tongue and red-stained lips puckered
    with his strawberried absence.

Rootless

No rooted tree ever felt safe to me.
When I was young, the neighbor kids
scaled the apple trees in the Knapps' backyard
or challenged a friendly trunked street maple.
But even at five or six I'd seen trees uprooted
by wind and water and never trusted their roots
to hold steady as I scrambled up one
or swung on uncertain branches.

My own family roots, too, brittle and frail,
cracked against that dry and rocky landscape
and never flourished in my native soil.
No surprise to me, then,
that I saw early they wouldn't hold
the weight of what I longed to be, and so to survive,
I cut loose and left that parched earth behind.
I secreted myself from what festered,
hid where I re-rooted then feasted on the rain
and nitrogen blazed from lightning strikes
that lit the land rippling with thunder
and echoing through clouds.
Replanted, I grew under skies that warmed with gentle sun
and finally I blossomed and shared my blooms.

Oh today, I still search memories of that scorched earth
and take with me seeds of what used to matter,
and now and then I plant some of those stunted hopes
in poems or stories I remember with wistful regret.

I cling to those wasted wisps of wisdom
handed down in saved letters or family stories
recited at my mother's table. Sometimes,
I even tend them, futilely hoping they might grow—
mutate to things I value—
and embedded as they are in my consciousness,
I still long for those dreams now-dead elders spun in tales—
"good old days" under a summer moon.

Post Script

*Even though I've never cared much for glossed over lies
and hand-me-down evasions, some things beg attention—
vines with their thorny dead branches may rattle
but still sculpt a sky with warning, and even though time
may not mend or polish a starkly broken tree limb,
dead wood floats and driftwood has its appeal.*

The Rain Within

Some days rain whispers a window, slow and steady—
not a storm that booms and rattles you nervous—
just a steady tap-tapping drizzle that slows your heart.

Such rain draws me to broken things—wings and promises,
opportunities missed, the injured and the lost.
Its chilly damp sends me fishing for smiles to warm the day.

Yes, I know its drizzled pulse, for I am walking wounded, too.
I've collected those badges of rejection and grief
issued by that tap, tapping rain that wears a heart down.

Have you ever felt that rain within you?

Part III:
Arching skyward, breathing free—untethered

Break-fast

I could not swallow
the tone of your voice
when it appeared over oatmeal,
tart and venomous.

Throughout the day, I held
back the bile, rising in gut-wrenching
tides and swamping the lowlands
where hope clung
until it became
anger-logged, then empty.

As afternoon waned
I knew I could never ingest
what you offered.
I packed your bags
and left them on the porch
beside an empty bowl.

All That Remains

An unfamiliar waitress asked,
"Are you a couple? Because you look
like you belong together."
—a still, small knot of fear
coiled within, wondered.
Then a chill in love fever.
Addiction? Lust?
What shuddered love?
Left it shaken? Stirred? Crushed?
Tossed on ice?

Your brother-in-law removed
all the liquor from his basement bar
but you booze-hound sniffed
some out in a drawer he missed.
I soloed to the Kentucky Derby,
placed promised bets, and you slept it off.
Home early to watch the run, I saw
you puking cherry-flavored schnapps.
"This was the end. I've done all I could."

Alanon—a door, a change, a path out.
No road map, no destiny divined—
just a hope floated me past doubt.
I worked myself whole, reshaped the clay:
counseled, divested denial, demanded reality,
and finally re-routed, repeated, stopped pretending—
until all paths led home.

All that remains is memory.

Divorce Decree: Untethered

Now that you are gone, I remember the cords of guilt
that lured me back when I wanted to soar.
Loosed, I am sky-driven, delighted in my wingspan,
captivated by the shadow I throw to earth.

I cannot say I miss those lines of blame,
though I sometimes long for connections.
Still the air, clear blue
or sweet with rain—
or even rigid with frosted clouds—
draws me more tightly
than the steel bands
once binding me to my lover's breast.
And so, I rise, shedding regrets,
arching skyward, breathing free—
untethered.

Closing the Door

The pain resonated, not when the door opened,
but when I finally closed it for good.
Hope cannot be banished
with just murmured prayers
because desire holds on to love long after
its flowers bloom, and its root dies.

Still, memory becomes mirror,
images diverge reflecting—
the comfort of our hands holding
as you drove South in sunshine
and the angles of anger
we imprinted later in snow-boot tracks.
Accusations through the years juxtaposed—
our ardor dressed in lies
we told ourselves
to justify our own betrayals.

(It took a while, but I finally let go
of that door-closing pain—
when I realized no answer brought understanding,
so no riddle of the heart was ever solved.
Even Hallmark could never script us back
to what we had.)

There I would embrace my peace:
I could not re-spark the passion
I felt for you in either of us,

but I could accept from you all that you vacated—
your daughter, your grandchildren,
and their love you left behind—
on that January day when you unexpectedly died.
I could make them mine, embrace them joyfully
and so I did—a cautionary tale
of what one might have lost to anger and delusion
but instead gained in forgiveness.

Let Them Go

I used to think love could mend hearts—
regenerate relationships' frayed edges,
and repair their ripped seams.
(When things no longer hold together,
shouldn't a beating heart
long for sutures to fill the holes?)
Scabbed dead ends, though,
and atrophy in understanding
don't restart hardened hearts.
So I learned to let go
and offer the gift of absence to those I once loved.
I've wished them peace in self-deception
and moved on to live my life—
one I can live with kindness
and without regret.

I need no fabrications, won't pose justifications,
flash indifference, or return cruelties.
I've quit waiting for realizations
and silenced my pleas for tolerance or love.
I now let them cocoon in their poisons,
even knowing no metamorphosis
will bloom for us any spring—
dead caterpillars don't grow butterflies.

Instead, my love waters other hopes—
coaxes them from their woven shelters
and feeds them as they thread lives worth living.
I hold onto those thriving hearts
and let papery shells of loveless souls
sift the wind, brittle and empty.

Unfinished Story

Sometimes grief darts before me,
on paths I would otherwise ignore.
It whispers directions on an errant breeze,
points the way to something buried.
When I'm lost, it speaks silence—
no happy echo of the past.
It lies unanswered like my prayers,
hollow and unholy.

Part IV:
Where the Twist Begins

Summer's Eve, Waiting for Rain

Sometimes on a summer's
eve, you can hear the thunder's
rumble creeping in, but you still gaze
at a star-studded sky hung with a sliver
of white-pie moon.
Under that canopy you inhale
deeply the moist, worm-scented
air. Rain will come;
you might feel it
in the stillness or in the warm
dampness of a clinging
shirt. You might even see
it in the distant flashes backlighting
the yard, but there, by the deck,
in the glow
spilling from the kitchen
window, the leaves are green
and the flowers poise
for sleep, serene and lovely.

Living in Limbo

Lazyboy-ed,
stretched back,
feet propped,
his eyes droop in almost sleep.
He peers at an early evening rerun,
Gunsmoke—
dreamscape of "wish-it-were,"
he'd longed for as a boy—
when everything was black and white,
and the good guys hung out
with Matt and Kitty
at the Long Branch.
In "wish-it-were,"
men belly up to the bar
to settle problems,
solvable in half-hour segments,
with a little help from Doc
or Festus
or Chester.

Still, what is, and what will be,
floats around him
in the high plains of maybe,
and maybe not.
His hand brushes his now-short frizz,
crispy in a 1950s buzz cut.

Everywhere else he's lost hair,
emasculated.
Lassoed,
tied down in blue tubing
by a stranger who rolled in
to perch under a window
and stayed,
humming and whispering
"What's to come?"
in a monotonous lisp,
he waits for Doc to ride in
with a bag of tricks
to heal what ails him,
or for Kitty to find a brew
to mute it all.
But in his land,
Matt can't jail the monsters
or finagle them out of town
or out-shoot them in a gunfight,
and when he honestly lays down his cards
and looks out the swinging doors
to the orange light on the horizon,
nothing growing
is the best he hopes for.

The Last Time We Made Love

The last time we made love,
I felt the death rattle of your lungs
vibrate against my hand.
I leaned into your chest,
felt your heartbeat stuttering.
At that moment I could not let go—
I held you long after you left my arms,
clung to those last gentle kisses,
those calloused palms caressing me,
the last thrusts that brought you to me.

I thought I could wrap you in memory of skin.
keep you in drumbeats of my heart,
find you throbbing on my fingertips.

Instead, you became the stuff of stars
a glitter of sky, a bit of light to wish upon—
something beyond my touch—
beyond the gravity of love.

Mourning in Michigan

The sun rises,
and he does not see it glint against snow.
He cannot inhale its sweet clarity.
I breathe in the day alone—
reluctantly prepared before he sped
to the sting of his setting sun.
Schooled in practicalities
of water lines and furnaces,
I stand alone, bereft
and unsuccored with what balms
might soothe an anguished heart.

Before, I've always found a wisp of courage
and had some hope to see me through.
This New Year, though, winds and twists with new losses
that wring such resilience from me.
Though I might envision where my paths might lead,
I question if I want even to trudge them.
Uncertain, I have paused
to fill my pockets with Christmas pebbles
I've gathered from beneath the snow.
In my grieving heart, they jangle a song of yesterday:
    I recall sweet bundles of candles scented with pine
    and days bubbling with Christmas cheer.
    Will remembrance fill the air with that peppermint?
    Or will it, instead, rattle me when much tarter sachets
    fragrance the air with his scent—
    oh, how can those prickly packages
    prod me on?

How can I leave this mourning—
cold and blunt as the snow he loved—
in Michigan?

Dispensation

You probably would not like
that I wear a ring
my first husband gave me.
I just sized it again—
an engagement ring
he surprised me with—
and I was lost in
a swirl of stony glitter,
a first-love whirlwind
as I whispered, "yes."

Back then I didn't even know to what.

Instead, you gave me flowers.
They poise around my deck
still blooming and swelling in the sun.
Clumped with bees and hornets
drawn to the sweetness
the rich savory sap,
they burst into hum of love
every summer day.

I guess I forgive you
for dying too young.

In the Memory of Skin

I keep a bottle of your cologne
in the drawer where you
kept your old toiletries.
On lonely days I pull it out,
untwist its cap,
and inhale its memory:

> *You stand leaning*
> *arms loose around me,*
> *looking down*
> *before you swoop in for a kiss*
> *then gather me close.*
> *I breathe the faint dampness beneath*
> *your shirt as you perspire*
> *in summer's heat; the air stirs*
> *Givenshy's π Neo and its scent*
> *hovers, completing the circle of us—*
> *our own haven—*
> *our world complete.*
> *There I feel the small moles of your*
> *shoulder tingle against my palm,*
> *stroke my fingers through*
> *the rough hair of your chest.*
> *I test its ripple of muscle beneath,*
> *and you stand solid and real against me*
> *tangled in the fragrance of days past.*

And I do not want to open my eyes
to let you disappear. So, for a while,
my yearning released from a bottle—
a wish granted to my heart—
is both enough and too little—
and then no more.

Empty Air: Epitaph

When the air empties of you,
and I no longer find your scent
in the flannel of your coat
hanging still in the garage;
when the shape of the trees you planted shifts
and I replace the coneflowers
withering without your touch;
when I rearrange the furniture
so I no longer look for you in your chair—
when I no longer cry when I open your drawers
to find socks neatly paired as you left them—
the ache of your absence will still throb in my bones,
as I look off the deck remembering
the shape of you in moonlight.

July 4, 2020

Outside, fireworks rumble under the July moon
then bloom against the sky above the trees.
In bursts of light and stars, memories and longings,
they crackle then spark against the night.
For the past few days, I've felt those flashes
of you surge into my heart,
and, as always, for brief moments,
it is as if you are still here by me
rapt in your own expectations.

And yet you are not.

You are buried deep in the town cemetery
where you wanted to be
under a stone that names us both
where my daughter will sprinkle my ashes
or leave them somewhere else to ride the wind.

Still, tonight, five years after you died,
I sit alone, though unlonely, in my own thoughts:
   Once we spent July 4 watching fireworks
   spill into a lake. We slipped inside to listen
   as explosives lit the sky. Perhaps our lips touched
   as we lay back on our bed,
   then basked in the rapture of other thunder.

In Memoriam: Christmas Greetings

Suspended in the space outside a snow-framed window,
grief floats above the sandy snowscape to comfort me.
On my couch trapped in the gravity of loss, I flip
calendar pages that once again counted down
another year without you.

Again, we will not share the lights of our Christmas tree
nor sample cookies I bake for Christmas Day.
I won't catch you stealing deviled eggs
from the trays I plan to take to parties.
And I know, even if that is all I'd want for Christmas,
I cannot bring you back.

So as you funnel down to that emptiness above the snow
and evaporate into the stars, look my way as you go.
Feel the pull of my love suspended in that inaccessible blankness
where once we touched, where I still embrace
what bridged us, and in the brightness of that light
wish me "Merry Christmas" once again.

On Layers of Grief

Where the twist begins is later in the poem,
but for now, I write only how we all write of sorrow.
I can package some feelings only in clichés.
The honesty blooms, however, with painful awareness:
the abuse caretakers suffer,
the cancer gripping him in its jaws.

(The poem till now reflects how everyone else saw it.
They didn't feel death reverberating in my husband's chest
or recall his cough resounding across Meijer Thrifty Acres
or remember that other cough ringing through my brain
that folded my father to a railing as he crossed
over the highway to parking near Briggs Stadium
or fear the loneliness of dreams cut short by funeral flowers.)

I didn't want that folded flag as a daughter,
and later, I didn't need to hear the title "widow"
or to feel the house's chilly echoes to know I was alone.
Yet the poem knows I was more than grateful
to retrieve some part of myself I had given up,
and that I enjoyed its homecoming,
as I buried the emptiness of caring
and thrust myself whole again into my own desires.

And here is that twist: that when I pivoted from love
that stole me from myself, that hid me from who I am,
I gave my sorrows voice, and set free,
I breathe.

What Lingers

She took your old-but-still-working truck
to her new job, taught her kids to drive in it,
loaned it to her husband when his jeep pooped out,
fetched groceries and birthday presents in it.

Whenever she drove it back to visit me,
our old cat Boguy slid outside to examine the tires,
sniffed each carefully to check where she'd been,
then returned to the house to rub against her legs,
purring in his approval.

*(Earlier, when I had given her your key fob,
its tinny metal and crackly plastic,
lingered in my finger memory—
a kind of scent or, perhaps, some imprint of you
that never wore off after you died.
I could hold it in my hand and remember
the warmth of your touch.
It felt like a smile from beyond the grave—
encouragement to hand your keys to someone
who would use your old truck to nurture others
the way you cared for our garden, our home, our lives—
me.)*

On Growing Older

I've lost track of heartbeats, and often can't find
the pulse of those I've loved. Now I cleave
to baskets of yesterdays they left dancing in wind gusts,
their wicker now loaded with flowers
and still swinging on my fall deck rail—
each rocks a memory to the beat
thumping gusts' erratic tunes—
as jarring as passing time.

Left on this lonely climb—
the ruins where we once counted stars,
forged laugh lines and carved our sighs on its paths—
I now climb alone, longing
for the comfort of those lost companions,
for the encouragement of their sharp tongues,
for the wisdom of those once-beating hearts,
even as their echoes marshal me forward.

Slow Waking

I like to wake up slowly,
then reach for my bedside book,
to read a chapter or two
before I present myself to realities
of hungry pets, and lists to drudge through
as the day grinds on.

Every morning, I hope to lie a moment in silence,
to hear my breath, mind my thoughts
recall memories and desires
before the plod of one foot
in front of another takes me to tasks
that buy presents for grandchildren,
do favors for in-laws, accompany friends
to appointments, get groceries for a weekend.

I sit up deliberately,
balance on the edge of the bed,
test the temperature of the room,
check the obstacles left on the floor—
shoes and clothes and cat toys—
then I stand, hoping to cover the distance
to the bathroom before my bladder wakes up.

After I've swallowed my handful of pills,
I remind myself each day how old I am
and that the day might not go as planned
when I discover on my journey
"what's not working today."

After, I take time to cuddle
and feed kitties weaving against my legs
then sit with a coffee cup, a pen
and some paper to write down a plan
or a poem before I wind my inner clock
with lists and goals that will spell down my day
like that moving hand, writing life.
I will cross off the items I've scribbled
in unremarkable print or bold or italics,
and daylight will dwindle down to night
as my life unravels to what matters.

Erasure Marks

I've been erasing you—
rubbing the traces of you
out of my life—
excising your memory.
Yesterday, I pulled your muscle shirts
from my drawer and placed them
in the donation bag.
You no longer accompany me
when I work out. In truth,
you haven't for a while.
Last week, I threw out
the Mr. and Mrs. address labels.
Since I've now shifted to the singles' table,
many of my friends today never met you.
Because it stopped working,
I'm debating repairing
or just replacing the grandmother clock
you gave me with something else.

It's not that I've stopped loving you,
but your chapters in my story have ended.
I've taken a different turn.
Yesterday, I drove through our town
thinking of how much has changed
since you died—how the world has shifted!

I'm so happy you spent so much of your time
here traveling life's road with me.
Now I travel lighter and design my routes
on roads you never ventured.
Don't worry, dear, I've heard
we end up in the same place,
even if we follow our own maps.

Alien Nation

We all arrive aliens,
walking lonely hearts,
inching, crawling,
toddling in tentative steps.
Looking for shelter,
we squirm into this unexpected world,
seeking relief from ourselves,
our landscapes, our paths.
It isn't a guest room we seek.
We scavenge for home,
for its warmth and for its solace—
a place to be ourselves—
enwombed, still whole, and at peace again.

About the Author

Mary Fox, a Detroit-born teacher and poet who grew up in Warren, MI, currently resides in Portland, MI. She graduated from Michigan State University (BA) and Central Michigan University (MS). She spent many years teaching at Fowler High School and at Lansing Community College.

Her books include the chapbooks *Waiting for Rain* (Finishing Line Press, 2016) and *Reading Lessons* (Finishing Line Press, 2019). She co-edited *Promptly Speaking* (2018), the fourth Writing at the Ledges anthology. Her work appears in various journals and anthologies, including both *Words Across the Water* from reading with Chicago and Lansing Poetry Clubs (2021, 2022), as well as 2024's Poetry Room anthology *Let's Go!*

In her spare time, she performs with several area organizations to promote poetry and encourage oral poetry as an art form. Coaching other poets in oral presentations and setting up poetry readings in area libraries afford her opportunities to share her love of poetry. Other organizations and venues with whom Mary collaborates and performs include: The Poetry Room, The Robin Theater, The Coffeehouse, and Writing at the Ledges. She finds helping others develop their poetic voices and promoting spoken-word are joyful experiences.

When she isn't writing, she enjoys swimming, attending plays and concerts, supporting social causes, socializing with friends and family, and reading.

www.ingramcontent.com/pod-product-compliance
Lightning Source LLC
Chambersburg PA
CBHW071121160426
43196CB00013B/2664